Connecticut
The Constitution State

Robin Koontz

PowerKiDS press™

New York

To my Connecticut friends, past and present

Published in 2011 by The Rosen Publishing Group, Inc.
29 East 21st Street, New York, NY 10010

First Edition

Editor: Amelie von Zumbusch
Book Design: Greg Tucker
Layout Design: Ashley Burrell
Photo Researcher: Jessica Gerweck

Photo Credits: Cover, pp. 9, 15, 17, 22 (bird and flower) Shutterstock.com; p. 5 Bruce Laurance/Getty Images; pp. 7, 9 (inset), 22 (Nathan Hale) © North Wind Picture Archives; p. 11 © www.iStockphoto.com/Denis Tangney Jr.; pp. 13, 22 (whale) Jen Kuhfs/Getty Images; p. 19 © Rudi Von Briel/age fotostock; p. 22 (tree) Wikimedia Commons; p. 22 (George W. Bush) Bob Levey/Getty Images; p. 22 (Stephenie Meyer) Steve Granitz/Wirelmage/Getty Images.

Library of Congress Cataloging-in-Publication Data

Koontz, Robin Michal.
  Connecticut : the Constitution State / Robin Koontz. — 1st ed.
      p. cm.
  Includes index.
  ISBN 978-1-4488-0647-8 (lib. bdg.) — ISBN 978-1-4488-0726-0 (pbk.) — ISBN 978-1-4488-0727-7 (6-pack)
  1. Connecticut—Juvenile literature. I. Title.
  F94.3.K66 2011
  974.6—dc22

2009047353

Manufactured in the United States of America

CPSIA Compliance Information: Batch #WS10PK: For Further Information contact Rosen Publishing, New York, New York at 1-800-237-9932

Contents

Welcome to Connecticut

The beautiful state of Connecticut is part of New England. New England is a group of states in the northeastern United States. Many people visit New England in the fall. They come to see the leaves change color from green to red, yellow, and orange. Connecticut's natural beauty makes it a great place to vacation. Along with colorful forests, the state has rocky hills and sandy beaches. Connecticut's southern edge is a coastline on Long Island Sound. The sound is part of the Atlantic Ocean.

Connecticut is also known for the useful things that were first made there. Some of the first **submarines**, can openers, and sewing machines were made in Connecticut. Toys, such as Silly Putty and Frisbees, were **invented** there.

This girl and her father are fishing in Westport, Connecticut. There are lots of fun things to do outside in beautiful Connecticut.

Early Beginnings

Thousands of Native Americans once lived in what is now Connecticut. The Indians hunted, fished, and traded with each other. In 1614, Dutch **explorers** came. They traded goods with the Indians. Soon after, English **colonists** arrived. The colonists fought with some of the nearby Indians. In the 1630s, the English and their Indian **allies** went to war with the Pequot Indians. The Pequot lost, and many were killed or captured.

In 1639, the colonists wrote the Fundamental Orders. It stated that the government would be run by leaders elected by the people. It was one of the earliest constitutions, or sets of laws saying how a government should be set up. This later earned Connecticut its nickname, the Constitution State.

The war between the Pequots and the English and their allies is known as the Pequot War.
This picture shows the English coming by boat to fight the Pequots.

Fighting with England

In 1662, the king of England signed a **charter**. It gave Connecticut's colonists certain rights. In 1687, England's new king tried to take the charter away. Then, the charter disappeared! Stories say that the colonists hid it in an oak tree. That tree became known as the Charter Oak.

By the 1700s, England had many colonies. The English taxed the colonists unfairly. Many people in 13 of England's colonies wanted to be independent. The two sides fought a war called the American Revolution. The people of Connecticut supplied the Colonial army with gunpowder, flour, and other goods. Colonial general George Washington called Connecticut the **Provisions** State. The colonists won the war and formed the United States.

Nathan Hale (inset) spied for the colonists in the Revolution. After being caught, he said "I only regret that I have but one life to lose for my country." His family home is in Coventry, Connecticut.

Mountains, Rivers, and Beaches

Connecticut is one of the smallest states. The state got its name from a Mohegan Indian word that means "beside the long **tidal** river." The Connecticut River flows south through the middle of the state. Connecticut also has lots of small rivers and waterfalls. It has more than 1,000 lakes, too. The state's biggest mountains and highest hills are in the northwest. In the northeast, the land has thick forests. Along the coast, there are low hills and beaches.

The weather in Connecticut is not that cold and not that hot. Though the state is small, the weather can be different in different parts of the state. Storms that make it snow in the north can cause light rain on the coast.

This lighthouse is on Connecticut's Fayerweather Island. Connecticut has several small islands off its southern coast.

Plants and Animals of the Past and Present

Huge dinosaurs once lived in Connecticut. You can see their footprints at Dinosaur State Park, in Rocky Hill, Connecticut. Today, animals such as raccoons and skunks live in Connecticut. Birds called purple martins live there, too. Trees, such as scarlet oaks and shagbark hickories, dot the landscape. Poison ivy also grows there. This plant can give people an itchy rash.

Connecticut's biggest animal is the sperm whale. It lives in the ocean off the southern shores. Sperm whales have big heads with round foreheads. They dive deep to hunt for food. The whales eat squid and fish. Connecticut whalers hunted sperm whales during the 1800s. Today, they are Connecticut's state animal.

Sperm whales live in oceans around the world. These huge whales were once widely hunted. Today, it is against the law to hunt them in most places.

Making Money in Connecticut

The early colonists of Connecticut were mostly farmers. However, there was not enough farmland for everyone to make money by farming. People started building factories. An inventor named Eli Whitney invented a gun that used **interchangeable** parts. He made machines to make the parts, too. Connecticut's factories still produce **military** supplies.

Today, banks and **insurance** companies are a big part of Connecticut's **economy**. **Universities**, such as Yale University, in New Haven, Connecticut, also provide jobs. In 1776, David Bushnell, a Yale student, invented the first submarine. Today, submarines are built in Groton, Connecticut. It is called the Submarine Capital of the World.

Yale University, seen here, has many beautiful buildings. Today, the school has about 11,000 students. Thousands of people work there, too.

A Beautiful Town

Hartford is the capital of Connecticut. Dutch traders arrived there in 1623. They built a trading post called House of Hope. In the 1630s, the English settled there. They named the town Hartford. The *Hartford Courant* was founded in 1764. This newspaper is still being produced today. The town is also home to the Wadsworth Athenaeum, the country's oldest public art **museum**.

By the 1790s, Hartford was an important city. Ships loaded goods from Hartford to sail to England and other far-away places. The shippers were afraid of things that could destroy their ships, such as storms and fires. Some of the shippers started the first American insurance company. Hartford is now known as the Insurance Capital of the World.

Hartford is home to the Connecticut State Capitol, seen here. Many members of the state's government work and meet there. The capitol overlooks the city's Bushnell Park.

Mystic Fun

Connecticut has lots of fun places to visit. One of these is the seaside town of Mystic. The town was a center for shipbuilding and whaling in the 1800s. Today, Mystic is known for its rich history. It is home to a living history museum, called Mystic Seaport. People can explore large sailing ships there. They can also see ships from the 1800s. Visitors watch as old ships are fixed up, too.

The Mystic Aquarium & Institute for Exploration is in Mystic, too. There, people can learn about animals that live in the ocean. Visitors can also learn about a sunken ship called the *Titanic*. Dr. Robert Ballard, who works for the Institute for Exploration, explored this ship.

Visitors to Mystic Seaport can see the *Charles W. Morgan*. This ship was built as a whaler, or a ship used on long trips to hunt whales. It first set sail in 1841.

The Greatest Show on Earth!

Connecticut's history is one reason that people visit the state. Some visitors learn about early American history. They walk through Colonial villages. People visit art museums and history museums, too. They can see cool things, such as the first helicopters and the first submarines.

One fun place to go is the P. T. Barnum Museum, in Bridgeport, Connecticut. In the 1800s, Barnum formed a circus. It was known as the Greatest Show on Earth. The museum has a huge model of the five-ring circus.

People also like to ski and snowboard in Connecticut. They play golf, too. They can fish, swim, and sail in the rivers, lakes, and sea. It is no wonder that lots of people are happy to live there!

Glossary

allies (A-lyz) Groups that stand together and help each other.

charter (CHAR-tur) An official agreement giving someone permission to do something.

colonists (KAH-luh-nists) People who move to a new place but are still ruled by the leaders of the country from which they came.

economy (ih-KAH-nuh-mee) The way in which a government oversees its goods and services.

explorers (ek-SPLOR-erz) People who travel and look for new land.

insurance (in-SHUR-ints) Protection against loss or harm.

interchangeable (in-ter-CHAYN-jeh-bel) Able to be used in place of something else.

invented (in-VENT-ed) Made something new.

military (MIH-luh-ter-ee) Having to do with the part of the government, such as the army or navy, that keeps its citizens safe.

museum (myoo-ZEE-um) A place where art or historical pieces are safely kept for people to see and to study.

provisions (pruh-VIH-zhunz) Food and supplies.

submarines (SUB-muh-reenz) Ships that are made to travel underwater.

tidal (TY-dul) Having to do with the daily rise and fall of the ocean.

universities (yoo-neh-VER-seh-teez) Schools people go to after high school.

Connecticut State Symbols

State Tree
Charter Oak

State Animal
Sperm Whale

State Flag

State Bird
American Robin

State Flower
Mountain Laurel

State Seal

Famous People from Connecticut

Nathan Hale
(1755–1776)
Born in Coventry, CT
Soldier and U.S. Spy

George W. Bush
(1946–)
Born in New Haven, CT
U.S. President

Stephenie Meyer
(1973–)
Born in Hartford, CT
Writer of the
Twilight books

Connecticut State Map

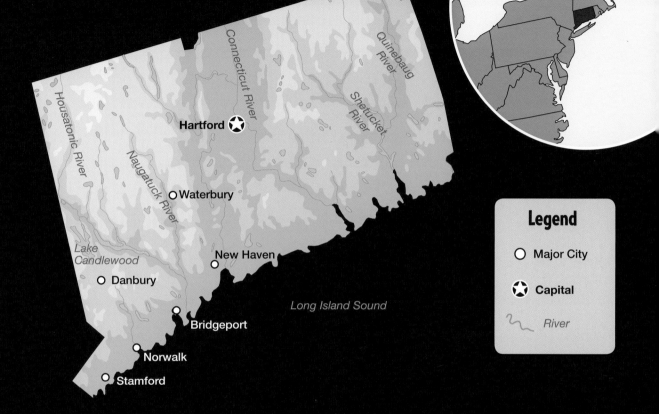

Housatonic River

Naugatuck River

Connecticut River

Quinebaug River

Shetucket River

Hartford ✪

○ Waterbury

Lake Candlewood

New Haven ○

○ Danbury

Long Island Sound

Bridgeport ○

Norwalk ○

Stamford ○

Legend

○ Major City

✪ Capital

〜 River

Connecticut State Facts

Population: About 3,405,565

Area: 5,018 square miles (12,997 sq km)

Motto: "Qui Transtulit Sustinet" ("He Who Transplanted Still Sustains")

Song: "Yankee Doodle"

Index

Web Sites

Due to the changing nature of Internet links, PowerKids Press has developed an online list of Web sites related to the subject of this book. This site is updated regularly. Please use this link to access the list:

www.powerkidslinks.com/amst/ct/